Illustrated by Gregory Green.
www.BlessedGraphix.net

I0058935

AFFIRMATIONS FOR PROSPERITY

"For I know the plans I have for you, "says the Lord. They are plans for good and not for disaster, to give you a future and a hope." (Jeremiah 29:11 NIV).

You should think of good things about yourself and conduct virtuous deeds. Search for good things, and good people, and develop smart habits because you deserve prosperity.

Affirmations for A Prosperous Mindset

26 ABC's
for Success and Wealth

Written by: Esther Johnson & Makayla Walker

(Forewords from professionals")

"Captivating, educational and inspiring" that describes this book. This God-ordained guide will cast light on to every child's pathway to financial freedom for generations to come. A timely message that is sure to bless youth of all ages, religions, and ethnicities. A great read that will build a legacy of financially sound leaders of tomorrow." Tamika R. Robison, Principal, Miami Dade Public Schools.

"I love this book for many reasons because it is well-written and gives great insight for children to understand. Kids friendly, and beautiful images which help them learn as well." Teresa Taylor, Guidance Counselor, Miami Dade Public Schools.

"This is an outstanding book that every young person should embrace because it prepares their mindset for greatness. I truly think this beautiful book is a beacon of light of their creativity and confidence to attain success." Synitheria Hilton, Elementary Teacher, Miami Dade Public Schools.

"A book well done and perfect for young children. I love it." Shirley Wilson, Parent, Retired Administrator

A

Abundance of love, peace, joy, kindness, and goodness belong to me.

B

Beauty is everywhere; I am beautiful and blessed for more blessings.

C

Confidence

and creativity live within, so I will create new things with confidence.

D

Diversification
in investing is
attainable and
sustainable for
me.

E

Education is the key to elevation and motivation for my life.

F

Freedom, financial happiness, and financial success are in my path.

G

Greatness and goodness always follow me.

H

Health and humility will forever be my lifestyle.

Increase and more increase must come in due season.

Jobs are a wonderful way to make money, so I will work and create jobs.

K

Knowledge is the principal thing, so I will gain wisdom.

L

Love is the greatest gift, so I will share my love with others.

M

Money is a tool that I will manage, monitor, and multiply.

N

New mindsets will drive my passion for success.

O

One step after the other will keep me going toward my goals.

P

Preparation will be essential for my designated success.

Q

Questions surrounding my future and finances should never cease.

R

Remember to save for my future while spending today.

S

Soak up knowledge surrounding my faith and finances.

T

Try to always control and monitor my finances.

U

Unveil ways for my family to receive wealth with me.

V

Venture to find ways my money can work for me.

W

Welcome new knowledge and information to learn and grow.

X

X-factor will be how people describe my money skills.

Y

Youth does not mean I should wait to save money and plan my career.

Z

Zeal for stability will always drive me to greatness.

About the Author

Esther Roundtree is the Founder, Young Excellent Scholar Academy LLC, and Y.E.S Finance Academy LLC, She is the Executive Director of a non-profit organization. She volunteers for Operation Hope, Youth for Christ, and Minister Wives Association.

A former teacher at Miami Dade Public Schools. After receiving calls from parents about their enthusiasm for her teaching economy (money skills) in the classroom, Mrs. Johnson had an epiphany to help solve an ongoing problem in underserved schools and communities. She grew up in poverty but shifted her mindset to prosperity, set financial goals and built generational wealth. Therefore, she decided to become an entrepreneur to educate, engage and elevate underserved children in financial literacy because they deserve financial education and financial success.

Currently, she is a certified vendor/contractor with Miami Dade Public Schools. She is elated about her shift from employee to employer.

Mrs. Johnson has been married to Dr. Carl Johnson since 1990; she has three young adults. She is a Minister, Mentor, Teacher, Real Estate Investor, and Financial Educator. Her passion is inspiring, influencing and impacting the lives of children and young adults to become smarter financially, spiritually, and academically. She has been featured in the Marquis Who's Who for her contributions to society.

For more information visit my website:

www.Yesacademy.miami
Email: YesacademyMiami@gmail.com
Instagram: Yes Academy Miami
Facebook: Yes Academy

ACKNOWLEDMENT

I would like to thank many of my sponsors, stakeholders, and supporters for giving me an opportunity to touch the hearts of children and families locally and globally. Miami Dade Public Schools, Director, Junor Anderson; Miami Dade County Government, Former Commissioner Jean Monestime; 93rd St. Community Development Corporation, President, Carl Johnson; Wells Fargo; The Children's Trust; Facebook; Barry University; Lotus House; and Miami Dade Public Schools. Students, parents, guardians, teachers, and principals for their participation and cooperation. National Financial Endowment and Association of Financial of Education & Planning for their scholarship and membership.

I am extremely grateful to my staff and volunteers for believing in my vision. Faith Johnson (Co-Founder) Isaiah Johnson, Shirley Wilson, Kourtney Montrope, Nathalie LaPorte, Ruby Hester, Debra Bartie, Denise Garrett-Stevens and Teresa Taylor.

Gregory Green is gifted with many talents to the world, he strives for perfection in every project that is assigned to him. He made this book perfect for children with his amazing illustrations. He is one of the best Graphic Designers, and I am so grateful that he's a part of my team.

I am profoundly grateful for everyone's overwhelming support in the mission to educate and engage underserved children and parents in financial literacy.

Thank you in advance for joining the movement to elevate the minds of children to hope for prosperity and peace.

Esther Johnson

www.ingramcontent.com/pod-product-compliance
Lightning Source LLC
Chambersburg PA
CBHW052046190326
41520CB00003BA/207